IF YOU WERE A
DOG

Clare Hibbert

W
FRANKLIN WATTS
LONDON • SYDNEY

First published in 2013 by Franklin Watts

Copyright © 2013 Arcturus Publishing Limited

Franklin Watts
338 Euston Road
London
NW1 3BH

Franklin Watts Australia
Level 17/207 Kent Street, Sydney, NSW 2000

Produced by Arcturus Publishing Limited,
26/27 Bickels Yard, 151–153 Bermondsey Street, London SE1 3HA

Editor: Joe Harris
Picture researcher: Clare Hibbert
Designer: Emma Randall

Picture credits:
All images Shutterstock except 5 (main) Ramona Richter/Tierfotoagentur/FLPA.

A CIP catalogue record for this book is available from the British Library.

Dewey Decimal Classification Number: 636.7

ISBN: 978 1 4451 1870 3

Franklin Watts is a division of Hachette Children's Books, an Hachette UK company.
www.hachette.co.uk

Printed in China

SL002675EN
Supplier 03, Date 0513, Print Run 2368

Contents

Sight, Sound and Touch

If you were a dog, you'd see and hear the world differently from humans. You would be better at finding your way around at dawn and dusk, when there is only faint light. You would also be able to pick up sounds that are outside the range of human hearing.

How dogs see

Cones are the parts of the eye's retina that sense colour and detail. Dogs have ten times fewer cones than us, and see the world in only blues and yellows. However, their retinas have more rods than ours. Rods are the parts of the retina that see the best in dim light.

Range of vision

Different breeds have different ranges of vision, depending on where the dog's eyes are on the head. A typical dog can see 250 degrees around its head, compared to a human's range of about 180 degrees.

Dog Questions

Q: Do dog whistles really work?
A: Dog whistles produce a sound that dogs can hear but humans can't. Dogs can hear twice the range of frequencies that humans can. They are better at hearing over distances, too – four times better than us!

Feelers

Dogs have whiskers around their muzzle and above their jaw. These feelers help dogs with their sense of touch and their 'spatial awareness' – for example, being able to tell if they can fit through a narrow gap.

A World of Smell

If you were a dog, you'd have a keen sense of smell. Your wild cousins, wolves, use smell for hunting, but you don't need to track down your food. You would use smell to check out your surroundings, to communicate with other dogs and even to sense people's emotions.

Super sniffers

A dog's sense of smell is far more impressive than a human's. A bloodhound's nose has around 230 million scent cells and a German shepherd's nose has 220 million. A person's nose has just five million scent cells.

Smelly messages

Dogs learn a lot about their surroundings through their noses. Out on a walk they are always pausing to sniff and find out which other dogs have been there, and whose territory they are in. Dogs mark their territory with strong-smelling urine and faeces.

Dog detectives

Dogs are brilliant at tracking so we use them to find missing people. They can pick up the 'trail' scent of someone lost, or a criminal on the run, even when it is days old. Dogs also help to find survivors after disasters.

Dog Questions

Q: Can dogs smell emotions?
A: Dogs can smell certain chemicals that people give off. For example, people (and dogs) secrete a hormone called cortisol when they are afraid.

Chasing and Herding

If you were a dog, you'd be a bundle of energy — keen to chase and track, and equipped with excellent senses to help you do just that. Your wild ancestors, wolves, herded animals when hunting as a pack, and you would have that instinct, too.

Champion speedsters

The fastest dogs — greyhounds and salukis — were bred to catch rabbits and hares. If they spot one, they cannot resist chasing it! They can race along at 60 kph (40 mph). Most dogs, though, are built for staying power, not speed.

Helpful herders

Some dogs have been bred to help farmers look after their livestock. Collies, sheepdogs, cattle dogs and mountain dogs all have a keen herding instinct and are intelligent, too. They can control sheep, goats or even cattle.

Sheepdog skills

At sheepdog trials, herding dogs can show off their skills. The exact challenges vary, but usually the dogs must drive the sheep around an obstacle course and into a pen, and also separate one or more animals from the rest.

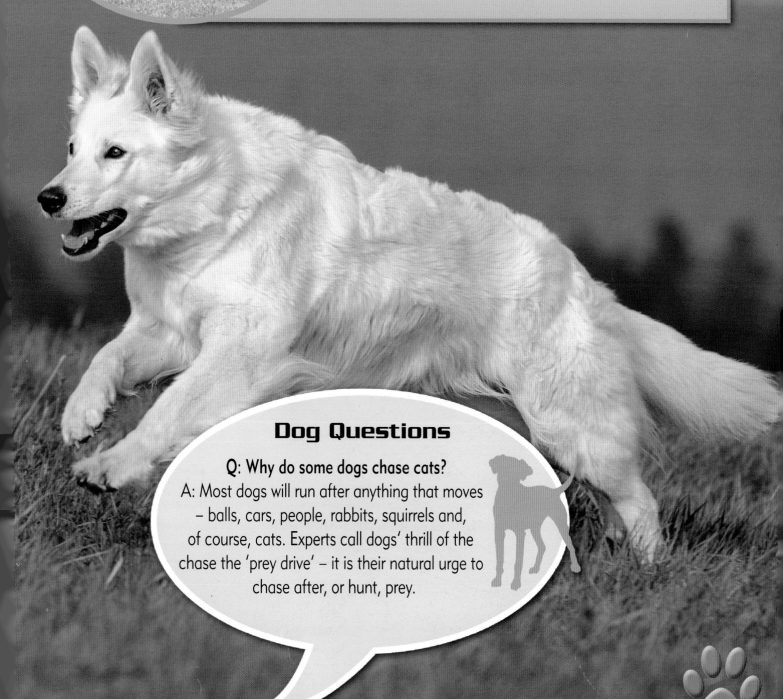

Dog Questions

Q: Why do some dogs chase cats?
A: Most dogs will run after anything that moves – balls, cars, people, rabbits, squirrels and, of course, cats. Experts call dogs' thrill of the chase the 'prey drive' – it is their natural urge to chase after, or hunt, prey.

Walkies!

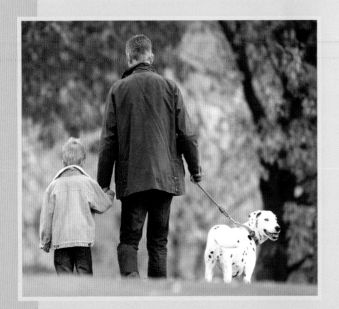

If you were a dog, going for a walk would be the highlight of your day. You would look forward to investigating interesting smells, finding fun things to chase and meeting other dogs. Best of all, you'd be spending time with your favourite companion – your owner!

Why walk?

Dogs need their daily exercise – and they love it, too. Many become terribly excited when they hear the word 'walk'! Some dogs even drop not-so-subtle hints, such as bringing their lead to their owner or standing by the door.

Meeting friends

Walks are social occasions. Along the route, dogs meet other dogs and greet them by sniffing their faces and bottoms. Dogs remember other individual dogs by their unique smell, not their appearance.

Running free

All dogs need to learn to walk calmly on a lead, but their favourite part of a 'walk' is when they can run free. Dogs' bodies are designed for long-distance running. Off the lead, dogs get the chance to really stretch their legs.

Pack Animal

If you were a dog, you would have descended from wolves. You would still share many characteristics with your wild cousins. You would be very sociable, and when you were running or playing with other dogs you would behave as if you were part of a pack.

Knowing their place

For many years, experts believed that dog owners should be like the 'top dog' of a wolf pack. Owners, they argued, should scold and punish dogs to help them understand their pack 'position' and be better behaved.

Training ideas

More recently, many experts have argued that relationships between pet dogs and people are different to those between wolves. Owners do not need to punish their pets into behaving well. Dogs respond better to rewards, praise and affection.

Pets away!

The close relationship between pet dogs and their owners means that dogs, unlike pet cats, can feel 'at home' anywhere. Going on holiday is an adventure for them – so long as their human family comes too.

Dog Questions

Q: What if a new dog joins the family?
A: Dog–dog relationships are different to dog–human ones, and closer to how wolves interact. When a new dog or puppy arrives, the animals must work out who is the 'top dog'.

Dog 'Talk'

If you were a dog, you'd be able to bark and make other noises. You would use these sounds to communicate. Your voice would allow you to demand things you needed or wanted, as well as to warn of danger or help those around you in other ways.

Barking

Dogs bark to sound the alarm. Pet dogs bark when they sense an intruder. In the wild, dogs do it to let other dogs know of approaching danger. Dogs also bark to challenge other dogs, or simply when they're overexcited.

Dog Questions

Q: Why does my dog growl when I give it a bone?
A: Dogs growl if they have something that they don't want to share. The sound sends a clear message: 'Back off and don't even think of trying to steal this treat from me!'

Howling

Wolves howl to communicate with each other over long distances. The pack can keep track of each other, and also communicate with other packs. Pet dogs howl to express worry or anxiety, for example, if their owners are away.

Whimpering

Puppies whimper as a sign of friendliness. Grown dogs will whimper for attention or to comfort themselves when they are lonely or in pain. Whining – the noise dogs make when they are begging – is different to whimpering.

Body Language

If you were a dog, your body language would be just as important for communicating as the noises you made. Your head, body and tail would all speak volumes – not only to other dogs, but also to the people around you. Body language would reveal your state of mind.

Tail talk

Dogs' tails are very expressive. Dogs wag them enthusiastically when they are feeling friendly and contented. Dogs that are doing things they enjoy, such as running or playing games, usually hold their tails upright.

Dog Questions

Q: Why does my dog lick my face?
A: Pups lick their mothers' faces to prompt them to regurgitate food, which the pups can eat. Dogs do the same to their owners, who are a bit like parents to them. They know their owners won't regurgitate food, though!

Threat display

Dogs can be very aggressive sometimes. When they want to frighten off a rival, they bare their teeth and stare their opponent in the eye. At the same time their hackles (neck hairs) rise.

The meek dog

Most dogs try to avoid getting into fights with bigger, more powerful dogs. The best way is to adopt a submissive pose. The signs of submission include ears moving back, eyes looking away and body and tail held low.

Dog Feelings

If you were a dog, you wouldn't feel the same all the time. You would react to events and to the emotions of those around you. Sometimes you'd feel grumpy, sometimes you might feel frightened and other times you would feel joyful and excited.

Feeling 'love'

Dogs long for human company and approval – but can this come from just anyone? It seems not. Pets pine for owners who die or go away, so doggy affection clearly amounts to more than just 'cupboard love'.

Scary stuff

Most dogs are frightened of thunderstorms and fireworks – they dislike the loud bangs and flashes of light. Dogs who are frightened flatten their ears, lower their tails and slink low to the ground.

Dog Questions

Q: Can dogs feel guilt?
A: Seventy-four per cent of dog owners think their dogs can feel guilt, but experts are not so sure. A 'guilty' dog avoids eye contact – behaviour that is more likely to be the dog trying to keep a low profile in response to the owner's mood.

18

Conquering fears
Sometimes dogs, especially rescue dogs, are fearful because they were mistreated in the past. With time and patience, their fears can usually be overcome, but some dogs may never feel secure in certain situations.

Training

If you were a dog, you'd be keen to learn and fit in. You would understand a range of basic commands. You would know what to do partly by recognizing the words themselves, but also by 'reading' your owner's tone of voice and body language.

Voice commands

The five basic commands for dogs are 'Sit', 'Stay', 'Come', 'Down' and 'Heel'. However, many dogs learn to recognize more instructions than these. The trick for the owner is to make each command sound as different as possible.

Rewards for obedience

Owners need to say their commands clearly so that their animals have a chance of understanding them. They should also reward good behaviour, either with a treat or with praising and patting.

Bad behaviour

Dogs are most likely to do things their owners don't want them to when they are bored. Clever owners avoid giving them the opportunity to misbehave. They make sure a space is 'dog-proof' before leaving their pet there unsupervised.

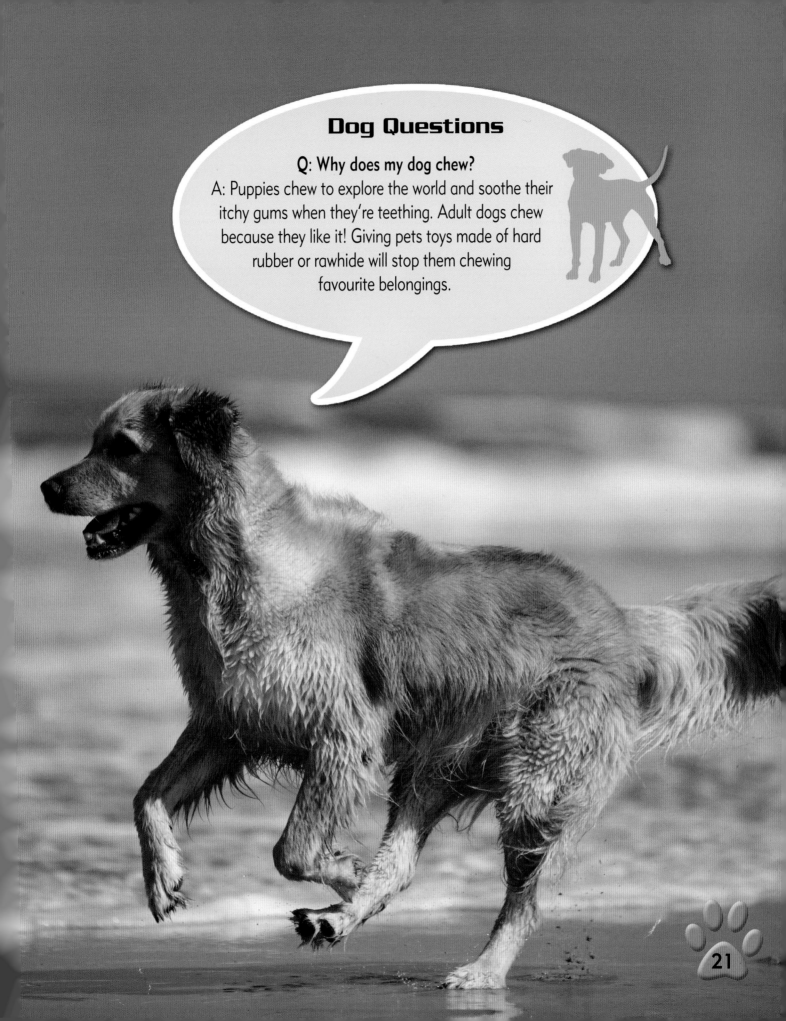

Dog Questions

Q: Why does my dog chew?
A: Puppies chew to explore the world and soothe their itchy gums when they're teething. Adult dogs chew because they like it! Giving pets toys made of hard rubber or rawhide will stop them chewing favourite belongings.

21

Meal Times

If you were a dog, you'd probably eat two meals a day. You'd prefer eating at the same times each day, so you knew when to expect your food. You'd also need fresh drinking water – about two-and-a-half times as much water, by volume, as food.

Doggy diet

Dogs are carnivores, or meat-eaters. They like nothing better than gnawing meat off a bone. Pet dogs get most of their meat from tinned food, which also contains cereals. Crunchy biscuits keep their teeth and gums healthy.

Dog Questions

Q: Is it okay to feed my dog between meals?
A: Obesity is a common problem for dogs – more than two-fifths of dogs in the United States are obese. Limiting food to mealtimes makes it easier to stop dogs overeating.

Teeth for the job

The four sharp teeth that wild dogs use to kill prey are called canines. (The word canine also means a member of the dog family.) At the back of the mouth, dogs have larger, flatter teeth that are good at tearing up flesh.

Taste

Dogs have only 1,700 taste buds, compared to a human's 9,000. Most are at the tip of the tongue. Dogs distinguish between bitter, sweet, salty and sour flavours – and like us, some dogs have a very sweet tooth!

Care for Fur

If you were a dog, you'd have a fur coat to keep you warm. You'd groom yourself by licking – and would have some help from your owner, too. You wouldn't be able to sweat, so if your cosy coat made you too hot, you'd pant to let heat escape and cool yourself down.

Hair styles

There are around 200 different breeds of dog, and many different hair styles. Dogs can have short, long, straight or curly fur. Fancy coats that are especially long or curly need lots of brushing and looking after.

Clean coats

Although dogs groom themselves, they also need help from their owners. Regular brushing helps to keep coats sleek, and strengthens the bond between owner and dog. Sometimes dogs will need bathing, too.

Dog Questions

Q: Why does my dog roll in smelly things?
A: Many dogs roll in fox faeces, rotting matter or other stinky stuff. They might do it to disguise their own scent from prey, or just because it's fun and they love strong smells!

Itching and scratching

A dog that is always scratching may have fleas. A vet can advise on the best way to stop fleas. Other parasites that can affect dogs include ticks (picked up on country walks) and worms.

Puppy Development

If you were a dog, you'd have started life as a puppy. You would have spent your first two or three months with your mother, who would have fed you milk and kept you warm and clean. While you were a puppy you'd have slept and played and learned the skills you'd need as a grown-up dog.

Newborns

At first, puppies just sleep and feed. They whimper and jostle for position. Their eyes and ears stay closed for the first couple of weeks. The only sense the pups need is smell – so they can sniff out their mother's milk.

Dog Questions

Q: Why does my puppy chase its tail?
A: Puppies love chasing games – they are good practice for hunting prey. If there are no brothers or sisters around to play chase with, a puppy will happily chase its own tail instead.

Litter mates

Small dogs may only have one or two puppies, but larger breeds may give birth to 20 or more. Playing with brothers and sisters is fun – and it teaches important life lessons, too, such as how to get along with others.

Feeding puppies

For the first three or four weeks, puppies only need milk. Then they can start to try solid food, such as biscuits. They carry on drinking their mother's milk, though, until they are weaned at six to eight weeks old.

Humans and Dogs

If you were a dog, you'd be used to getting along with humans — dogs have been doing so since they were first domesticated thousands of years ago. You'd be loyal to your owner and you might even work as a companion for a living!

Workers and companions

Early humans found dogs useful because they helped them to hunt. People still use dogs as guard dogs or hunting dogs. Although they take on responsible jobs, dogs can be playful too. Even an adult dog will adopt a puppyish pose when it wants to play.

Dog Questions

Q: How should I approach a strange dog?
A: Dogs are usually friendly, but it's not a good idea to approach a dog you don't know. Ask its owner first. If they say it's okay, then you can crouch low, and offer your hand for the dog to sniff.

Assistance dogs

Dogs make great helpers. Some are trained to assist people who are blind, deaf or in a wheelchair. Their amazing ability to smell chemical changes means dogs can even forewarn owners with epilepsy when they are about to have a seizure.

Responsibilities

Dogs are part of the family. They live for 15 years or more and owners have to care for them all that time – feeding them, walking them and taking them to the vet. To prevent unwanted puppies, owners should also have their dogs neutered.

Glossary

ancestor A member of the family that lived long ago.

anxiety Worry. Some dogs suffer 'separation anxiety' – stress when they are separated from their owners, for example when they are out at work or school.

breed A class of dogs that look similar and have related ancestry, for example golden retriever.

carnivore An animal whose diet is mostly meat. Most carnivorous mammals have four long, sharp teeth near the front of the mouth (canines) that are designed for tearing through flesh.

'cupboard love' Affection that is faked in order to get something, such as food.

domesticated Describes an animal that is used to living alongside people, rather than in the wild.

epilepsy A condition that means sufferers sometimes lose consciousness or have convulsions (a seizure).

hackles Hairs on the back of a dog's neck that stand up when the animal is angry or alarmed.

hormone A substance released into the blood by a gland that changes how certain body cells behave. Cortisol is a hormone released by people and dogs when they are afraid.

livestock Animals kept by farmers, such as cattle, sheep and pigs.

muzzle The protruding part of an animal's face that includes the nose and mouth.

neutered Describes an animal that has had an operation to remove its reproductive organs so that it cannot have young.

obese Extremely overweight – in dogs, obesity means being about 15 per cent heavier than their ideal bodyweight.

parasite An animal that lives on another animal and relies on it for food.

pine for Miss and long for.

prey An animal that is hunted by other animals for food. Rabbits are typical prey for wild dogs.

regurgitate Spit up partly-chewed food. Mother dogs regurgitate meat for their puppies.

responsibility A task that someone has to perform as part of their job, or because of their relationship to someone else.

retina The light-sensitive lining at the back of the eye that allows an animal to see.

scent cells Receptors in the nose that send signals to the brain, which then makes sense of that information allowing an animal to smell.

spatial awareness The ability to sense what is in the surrounding space.

submissive Meek.

taste buds Receptors in the mouth that send signals to the brain, which then makes sense of that information, allowing an animal to taste.

territory The area of land where an animal lives. Dogs mark their territory with urine or faeces.

weaned Taken off mother's milk and put exclusively on to solid foods.

Further Reading

100 Things You Should Know About: Dogs and Puppies by Camilla de la Bedoyere (Miles Kelly Publishing, 2006)

Complete Puppy and Dog Care by Bruce Fogle (Mitchell Beazley, 2010)

How to Speak Dog! by Sarah Whitehead (A&C Black, 2007)

Understanding Your Dog: The First Guide for Humans Written by a Dog by Sue Day (CreateSpace Independent Publishing Platform, 2011)

Websites

animal.discovery.com/guides/dogs/dogs.html
A guide to dog care from the Animal Planet website, with information on choosing a dog, dog life stages, dog health and dog-proofing your home.

www.loveyourdog.com
A kids' guide to dog care, including tips on training.

www.rspca.org.uk/allaboutanimals/pets/dogs
A guide to looking after your dog from the animal care charity, the RSPCA.

www.squidoo.com/the-a-to-z-guide-to-dogs-for-kids-of-all-ages
An A-to-Z guide to dog breeds.

www.the-kennel-club.org.uk
The official website for the Kennel Club, a UK organization that gives information and advice to dog owners.

Index

Series Contents

If You Were a Cat How Cats Hunt • Cats' Eyes • Amazing Senses • Contented Cats • Grumpy Cats • Body Language • The Home Range • How Cats Move • Caring for Fur • Cat Food • Kittens • Cat Breeds • Humans and Cats

If You Were a Dog Sight, Sound and Touch • A World of Smell • Chasing and Herding • Walkies! • Pack Animal • Dog 'Talk' • Body Language • Dog Feelings • Training • Meal Times • Care for Fur • Puppy Development • Humans and Dogs

If You Were a Dolphin Dolphins and Whales • Hunting for Food • Echolocation • Hearing and Seeing • Touch and Taste • Brains and Intelligence • Communication • Family Life • Where Dolphins Live • How Dolphins Breathe • Swimming • Dolphin Babies • People and Dolphins

If You Were a Horse Horse Senses • Horse Eyes • Ears and Hearing • Body Language • Horse Talk • Friendship • Feeding • Grooming • Running Free • Resting • Mother and Foal • Working Horses • Horse and Rider

If You Were a Shark All Kinds of Shark • Shark Teeth • Sight and Sound • Smell, Taste and Touch • Super Senses • On the Move • Shark Tails • Maneaters • Pack Hunters • Filter Feeders • Migration • Shark Babies • A Very Strange Family

If You Were a Snake Seeing and Hearing • Super Senses • Hunting Tricks • Constrictors • Venomous Snakes • Feeding • How Snakes Move • Swimming Snakes • Snake Talk • Snake Defences • Snake Skin • Baby Snakes • Where Snakes Live